all of it

Alistair McDowall

T0347842

methuen | drama

LONDON • NEW YORK • OXFORD • NEW DELHI • SYDNEY

METHUEN DRAMA
Bloomsbury Publishing Plc
50 Bedford Square, London, WC1B 3DP, UK
1385 Broadway, New York, NY 10018, USA

BLOOMSBURY, METHUEN DRAMA and the Methuen Drama logo are
trademarks of Bloomsbury Publishing Plc

First published in Great Britain 2020

For legal purposes the Acknowledgements on p. vii
constitute an extension of this copyright page.

Cover design: Ben Anslow

Cover image © Michael Burrell / Alamy Stock Photo

All rights whatsoever in this play are strictly reserved and application for
performance etc. should be made before rehearsals by professionals and by
amateurs to Judy Daish Associates, 2 St Charles Place, London, W10 6EG.
No performance may be given unless a licence has been obtained.

No rights in incidental music or songs contained in the work are hereby
granted and performance rights for any performance/presentation
whatsoever must be obtained from the respective copyright owners.

A catalogue record for this book is available from the British Library.

A catalog record for this book is available from the Library of Congress.

ISBN: PB: 978-1-3501-6816-9
ePDF: 978-1-3501-6817-6
eBook: 978-1-3501-6818-3

Series: Modern Plays

Typeset by Mark Heslington Ltd, Scarborough, North Yorkshire

To find out more about our authors and books visit
www.bloomsbury.com and sign up for our newsletters.

THE ROYAL COURT THEATRE PRESENTS

all of it

by Alistair McDowall

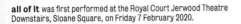

all of it was first performed at the Royal Court Jerwood Theatre Downstairs, Sloane Square, on Friday 7 February 2020.

all of it
by Alistair McDowall

Performed by
Kate O'Flynn

Director **Vicky Featherstone**
Lighting Designer **Anna Watson**
Sound Designer **David McSeveney**
Assistant Director **Izzy Rabey**
Casting Director **Amy Ball**
Production Manager **Marius Rønning**
Costume Supervisor **Lucy Walshaw**
Stage Manager **Charlotte Padgham**

The Royal Court Theatre and Stage Management wish to thank the following for their help
with this production:
Chloe for the stool, from all of us.

all of it
by Alistair McDowall

Alistair McDowall (Writer)

For the Royal Court: **X, Talk Show (Open Court).**

Other theatre includes: **Zero for the Young Dudes!** (NT Connections); **Pomona (Orange Tree/ National/Royal Exchange, Manchester); Brilliant Adventures (Royal Exchange, Manchester/Live, Newcastle); Captain Amazing (Live, Newcastle/Edinburgh Festival Fringe/ UK tour).**

Vicky Featherstone (Director)

For the Royal Court: **On Bear Ridge [co-director] (& National Theatre Wales), The Cane, Gundog, My Mum's a Twat [co-director], Cyprus Avenue (& Abbey, Dublin/Public, NYC), Bad Roads, Victory Condition, X, How to Hold Your Breath, God Bless the Child, Maidan: Voices from the Uprising, The Mistress Contract, The Ritual Slaughter of Gorge Mastromas; Untitled Matriarch Play, The President Has Come to See You (Open Court Weekly Rep).**

Other theatre includes: **What If Women Ruled the World?** (Manchester International Festival); **Our Ladies of Perpetual Succour (& National/ West End/International tour), Enquirer [co-director], An Appointment with the Wicker Man, 27, The Wheel, Somersaults, Wall of Death: A Way of Life [co-director], Cockroach (& Traverse), 365 (& Edinburgh International Festival), Mary Stuart (& Citizens/Royal Lyceum, Edinburgh), The Wolves in the Walls [co-director] (& Tramway/Lyric, Hammersmith/UK tour/New Victory, NYC), The Miracle Man, Empty, Long Gone Lonesome (National Theatre of Scotland); The Small Things, Pyrenees, On Blindness, The Drowned World, Tiny Dynamite, Crazy Gary's Mobile Disco, Splendour, Riddance, The Cosmonaut's Last Message to the Woman He Once Loved in the Former Soviet Union, Crave (Paines Plough).**

Television Includes: **Pritilata (from Snatches: Moments from 100 Years of Women's Lives), Where the Heart Is, Silent Witness.**

Film includes: **Climate Change: what do you want me to say? (Royal Court/Financial Times short film), Cyprus Avenue (The Space/BBC capture).**

Vicky was Artistic Director of Paines Plough 1997-2005 and the inaugural Artistic Director of the National Theatre of Scotland 2005-2012. She is Artistic Director of the Royal Court.

David McSeveney (Sound Designer)

For the Royal Court: **Cyprus Avenue (& Abbey, Dublin/Public, NYC), The Cane, Girls & Boys (& Minetta Lane, NYC), Father Comes Home from the Wars (Parts 1, 2 & 3), Open Court 2016, Lela & Co., Constellations (& West End/Broadway/ UK tour), Teh Internet Is Serious Business, The Art of Dying, Not I/Footfalls/Rockaby (& West End/UK & International tour), The Djinns of Eidgah, Routes, If You Don't Let Us Dream We Won't Let You Sleep, Belong, Vera Vera Vera, The Village Bike, Clybourne Park (& West End), Ingredient X, Posh (& West End), Disconnect, Cock, A Miracle, The Stone, Shades, Seven Jewish Children, The Girlfriend Experience (& Theatre Royal, Plymouth/Young Vic), Contractions, Fear & Misery/War & Peace.**

Other theatre includes: **The Skriker (Manchester International Festival/Royal Exchange, Manchester); Blurred Lines (National); A Doll's House (& West End/BAM, NYC), Macbeth, The Changeling (Young Vic); Wolf in Snakeskin Shoes, Stones in His Pockets (Kiln); The Duke in Darkness, Tryst, Sexy Laundry (Tabard); The Winter's Tale (RSC); Victoria Station/One for the Road (Print Room/Young Vic); On the Record (Arcola); The Tin Horizon (Theatre503); Gaslight (Old Vic); Charley's Aunt, An Hour & a Half Late (Theatre Royal, Bath); A Passage to India, After Mrs Rochester, Madame Bovary (Shared Experience); Men Should Weep, Rookery Nook (Oxford Stage Company); Othello (Southwark).**

David is Head of Sound at the Royal Court.

Kate O'Flynn (Performer)

For the Royal Court: **the end of history..., Anatomy of a Suicide, The Ritual Slaughter of Gorge Mastromas, A Miracle.**

Other theatre includes: **[BLANK] (Donmar); One for the Road/Mountain Language/Ashes to Ashes (West End); The Glass Menagerie (West End/Edinburgh International Festival); The Trial (Young Vic); A Taste of Honey, Port (National); Lungs, The Sound of Heavy Rain (Paines Plough/Crucible, Sheffield); Marine Parade (ETT); The Whisky Taster (Bush); House of Special Purpose (Chichester Festival); See How They Run, The Children's Hour (Royal Exchange, Manchester).**

Television includes: **Brexit, No Offence, Wanderlust, Doctor Thorne, Not You Again, Ordinary Lies, New Tricks, Room at the Top, Playhouse Presents: The Snipist, Above Suspicion, The Syndicate, The Suspicions of Mr Whicher, Kingdom, The Palace, Trial & Retribution.**

Film includes: **Peterloo, Bridget Jones' Baby, Mr. Turner, Up There, Happy Go Lucky.**

Awards include: **Clarence Derwent Award for Best Female in a Supporting Role (The Glass Menagerie); Manchester Evening Standard Award for Best Newcomer, TMA Award for Best Supporting Actress (The Children's Hour); Critics' Circle Award for Most Promising Newcomer (Port).**

Izzy Rabey (Assistant Director)

For the Royal Court: **On Bear Ridge (& National Theatre Wales).**

As director, other theatre includes: **TYFU: Welsh Writers Project (Theatr Clwyd/Pains Plough); Hang (Run Amok/The Other Room); Under the Sofa [part of Chippy Lane Productions: An Evening of Welsh Playwrights] (Bloomsbury Festival); Flowers of the Dead Red Sea (Run Amok/Aberystwyth Arts Centre/RWCMD/The Rosemary Branch); 4:48 Psychosis (Run Amok/Aberystwyth Arts Centre/Chapter Arts Centre).**

As assistant director, other theatre includes: **Land of My Fathers (Lurking Truth/Aberystwyth Arts Centre); Play/Silence (The Other Room).**

Izzy is a Trainee Director at the Royal Court.

Anna Watson (Lighting Designer)

For the Royal Court: **Poet in da Corner (& UK tour), Pity, You for Me for You, Plaques & Tangles, A Time to Reap.**

Other theatre includes: **Appropriate, Becoming: Part One, Salt Root & Roe (Donmar); Henry VI, Richard III [as candlelight consultant] (Sam Wanamaker); Gaslight (Watford Palace); Christmas Carol (Bristol Old Vic); Leave to Remain, The seagull, Shopping & Fucking (Lyric, Hammersmith); The Fantastic Follies of Mrs Rich, Snow in Midsummer, The Roaring Girl (RSC); Twilight: Los Angeles 1992, The Chronicles of Kalki (Gate); Box of Delights (Wilton's Music Hall); King Lear (Globe); Dutchman, The Secret Agent, Fireface, Disco Pigs, Sus (Young Vic); Bank on it (Theatre-Rites/Barbican); On the Record, it felt empty when the heart went at first but it is alright now (Arcola); Paradise, Salt (Ruhr Triennale, Germany); Gambling, This Wide Night (Soho); Rutherford & Son, Ruby Moon (Northern Stage); ...Sisters (Headlong); King Pelican, Speed Death of the Radiant Child (Drum, Plymouth).**

Dance includes: **Mothers, Soul Play (The Place); Refugees of a Septic Heart (The Garage); View from the Shore, Animule Dance (Clore ROH).**

Opera includes: **Don Carlo (Grange Park); Orlando (WNO/Scottish Opera/San Francisco); Cendrillon (Gyndebourne); Ruddigore (Barbican/Opera North/UK Tour); Critical Mass (Almeida); Songs from a Hotel Bedroom, Tongue Tied (Linbury ROH); The Bartered Bride (Royal College of Music); Against Oblivion (Toynbee Hall).**

THE ROYAL COURT THEATRE

The Royal Court Theatre is the writers' theatre. It is a leading force in world theatre for cultivating and supporting writers – undiscovered, emerging and established.

Through the writers, the Royal Court is at the forefront of creating restless, alert, provocative theatre about now. We open our doors to the unheard voices and free thinkers that, through their writing, change our way of seeing.

Over 120,000 people visit the Royal Court in Sloane Square, London, each year and many thousands more see our work elsewhere through transfers to the West End and New York, UK and international tours, digital platforms, our residencies across London, and our site-specific work. Through all our work we strive to inspire audiences and influence future writers with radical thinking and provocative discussion.

The Royal Court's extensive development activity encompasses a diverse range of writers and artists and includes an ongoing programme of writers' attachments, readings, workshops and playwriting groups. Twenty years of the International Department's pioneering work around the world means the Royal Court has relationships with writers on every continent.

Within the past sixty years, John Osborne, Samuel Beckett, Arnold Wesker, Ann Jellicoe, Howard Brenton and David Hare have started their careers at the Court. Many others including Caryl Churchill, Athol Fugard, Mark Ravenhill, Simon Stephens, debbie tucker green, Sarah Kane – and, more recently, Lucy Kirkwood, Nick Payne, Penelope Skinner and Alistair McDowall – have followed.

The Royal Court has produced many iconic plays from Lucy Kirkwood's **The Children** to Jez Butterworth's **Jerusalem** and Martin McDonagh's **Hangmen**.

Royal Court plays from every decade are now performed on stage and taught in classrooms and universities across the globe.

It is because of this commitment to the writer that we believe there is no more important theatre in the world than the Royal Court.

🐦 royalcourt ⬛ royalcourttheatre

Supported using public funding by
ARTS COUNCIL ENGLAND

ROYAL

COMING UP AT THE ROYAL COURT

4 – 21 Mar

Shoe Lady
By E.V. Crowe

2 – 25 Apr

Rare Earth Mettle
By Al Smith

Generously supported with a lead gift from Charles Holloway. Recipient of an Edgerton Foundation New Play Award. Supported by Cockayne Grant for the Arts, a donor advised fund of The London Community Foundation.

9 Apr – 9 May

two Palestinians go dogging
By Sami Ibrahim

Royal Court Theatre and Theatre Uncut

7 – 16 May

The Song Project
Concept by Chloe Lamford and Wende

Created by Chloe Lamford, Wende, Isobel Waller-Bridge and Imogen Knight

With words by E.V. Crowe, Sabrina Mahfouz, Somalia Seaton, Stef Smith and Debris Stevenson

20 May – 20 Jun

A Fight Against...
By Pablo Manzi

Translated by William Gregory

Royal Court Theatre and Teatro a Mil Foundation The development of A FIGHT AGAINST... was supported by the British Council.

29 May - 3 Jul

The Glow
By Alistair McDowall

29 Jun - 11 Jul

Purple Snowflakes and Titty Wanks
By Sarah Hanly

Royal Court Theatre and Abbey Theatre

20 Jul - 15 Aug

Is God Is
By Aleshea Harris

royalcourttheatre.com

Sloane Square London, SW1W 8AS
⊖ Sloane Square ⇌ Victoria Station
🐦 royalcourt 📘 theroyalcourttheatre 📷 royalcourttheatre

ASSISTED PERFORMANCES

Captioned Performances

Captioned performances are accessible for D/deaf, deafened & hard of hearing people as well as being suitable for people for whom English is not a first language. There are regular captioned performances in the Jerwood Theatre Downstairs on Wednesdays and the Jerwood Theatre Upstairs on Fridays.

In the Jerwood Theatre Downstairs
Shoe Lady: Wed 18 Mar, 7.30pm
Rare Earth Mettle: Wed 22 Apr, 7.30pm
The Glow: Wed 17, 24 Jun & 1 July, 7.30pm
Is God Is: Wed 5 & 12 Aug, 7.30pm

In the Jerwood Theatre Upstairs
two Palestinians go dogging: Fri 24 Apr, 1 & 8 May, 7.45pm
A Fight Against...: Fri 5, 12 & 19 Jun, 7.45pm

Audio Described Performances

Audio described performances are accessible for blind or partially sighted customers. They are preceded by a touch tour (at 1pm) which allows patrons access to elements of theatre design including set and costume.

In the Jerwood Theatre Downstairs
Shoe Lady: Sat 21 Mar, 2.30pm
Rare Earth Mettle: Sat 25 Apr, 2.30pm
The Glow: Sat 27 Jun, 2.30pm
Is God Is: Sat 8 Aug, 2.30pm

There will be a touch tour (at 1pm) and enhanced pre-show notes for
Poet in da Corner on Sat 22 Feb, 2.30pm

ROYAL

ASSISTED PERFORMANCES

Performances in a Relaxed Environment

Relaxed Environment performances are suitable for those who may benefit from a more relaxed experience.

During these performances:
There will be a relaxed attitude to noise in the auditorium; you are
welcome to respond to the show in whatever way feels natural
You can enter and exit the auditorium when needed
We will help you find the best seats
House lights remained raised slightly
Loud noises may be reduced

In the Jerwood Theatre Downstairs
Rare Earth Mettle: Sat 18 Apr, 2.30pm
The Glow: Sat 13 Jun, 2.30pm
s God Is: Sat 1 Aug, 2.30pm

In the Jerwood Theatre Upstairs
two Palestinians go dogging: Sat 2 May, 3pm
A Fight Against...: Sat 20 Jun, 3pm

If you would like to talk to us about your access requirements please contact our Box Office at (0)20 7565 5000 or **boxoffice@royalcourttheatre.com**
The Royal Court Visual Story is available on our website. We also produce Story Synopsis and Sensory Synopsis which are available on request.

For more information and to book access tickets online, visit

royalcourttheatre.com/access

Sloane Square London, SW1W 8AS ⊖ Sloane Square ⇄ Victoria Station
🐦 royalcourt 🅵 theroyalcourttheatre 📷 royalcourttheatre

ROYAL COURT SUPPORTERS

The Royal Court is a registered charity and not-for-profit company. We need to raise £1.5 million every year in addition to our core grant from the Arts Council and our ticket income to achieve what we do.

We have significant and longstanding relationships with many generous organisations and individuals who provide vital support. Royal Court supporters enable us to remain the writers' theatre, find stories from everywhere and create theatre for everyone.

We can't do it without you.

PUBLIC FUNDING

Arts Council England, London
British Council

TRUSTS & FOUNDATIONS

The Derrill Allatt Foundation
The Backstage Trust
The Boshier-Hinton Foundation
Martin Bowley Charitable Trust
The Chapman Charitable Trust
CHK Foundation
The City Bridge Trust
The Cleopatra Trust
Cockayne - Grants for the Arts
The Ernest Cook Trust
The Nöel Coward Foundation
Cowley Charitable Trust
The D'oyly Carte Charitable Trust
Edgerton Foundation
The Eranda Rothschild Foundation
Lady Antonia Fraser for The Pinter Commission
The Golden Bottle Trust
The Haberdashers' Company
The Paul Hamlyn Foundation
Roderick & Elizabeth Jack
Jerwood Arts
The Leche Trust
The Andrew Lloyd Webber Foundation
The London Community Foundation
John Lyon's Charity
Clare McIntyre's Bursary
The Austin & Hope Pilkington Trust
Old Possum's Practical Trust
The David & Elaine Potter Foundation
The Richard Radcliffe Charitable Trust
Rose Foundation
Royal Victoria Hall Foundation
The Sobell Foundation
Span Trust
John Thaw Foundation
The Garfield Weston Foundation
The Victoria Wood Foundation

CORPORATE SPONSORS

Aqua Financial Limited
Cadogan
Colbert
Edwardian Hotels, London
Fever-Tree
Greene King
Kirkland & Ellis International LLP
Kudos
MAC

CORPORATE MEMBERS

Platinum
Auriens
Lombard Odier

Gold
Weil, Gotshal & Manges LLP

Silver
Azteca Latin Lounge
Bloomberg
Kekst CNC
Left Bank Pictures
The No 8 Partnership Dental Practice
PATRIZIA
Royal Bank of Canada - Global Asset Management
Tetragon Financial Group

COMMISSION PARTNERS
Oberon Books

For more information or to become a foundation or business supporter contact: support@royalcourttheatre. com/020 7565 5064.

Supported using public funding by
ARTS COUNCIL
ENGLAND

ROYAL

BAR & KITCHEN

The Royal Court's Bar & Kitchen aims to create a welcoming and inspiring environment with a style and ethos that reflects the work we put on stage. Our menu consists of simple, ingredient driven and flavour-focused dishes with an emphasis on freshness and seasonality. This is supported by a carefully curated drinks list notable for its excellent wine selection, craft beers and skilfully prepared coffee. By day a perfect spot for long lunches, meetings or quiet reflection and by night an atmospheric, vibrant meeting space for cast, crew, audiences and the general public.

GENERAL OPENING HOURS
Monday – Friday: 10am – late
Saturday: 11am – late

Advance booking is suggested at peak times.

For more information, visit

royalcourttheatre.com/bar

HIRES & EVENTS

The Royal Court is available to hire for celebrations, rehearsals, meetings, filming, ceremonies and much more. Our two theatre spaces can be hired for conferences and showcases, and the building is a unique venue for bespoke weddings and receptions.

For more information, visit

royalcourttheatre.com/events

Sloane Square London, SW1W 8AS ⊖ Sloane Square ⇄ Victoria Station
🐦 royalcourt 🄵 theroyalcourttheatre 📷 royalcourttheatre

COURT

"There are no spaces, no rooms in my opinion, with a greater legacy of fearlessness, truth and clarity than this space."

Simon Stephens, Playwright

The Royal Court invests in the future of the theatre, offering writers the support, time and resources to find their voices and tell their stories, asking the big questions and responding to the issues of the moment.

As a registered charity, the Royal Court needs to raise at least £1.5 million every year in addition to our Arts Council funding and ticket income, to keep seeking out, developing and nurturing new voices. Please join us by donating today.

You can donate online at **royalcourttheatre.com/donate** or via our **donation box in the Bar & Kitchen.**

We can't do it without you.

Support the Court

To find out more about the different ways in which you can be involved please contact support@royalcourttheatre.com/ 020 7565 5049

all
      of
   it

to be spoken aloud by one performer,
quickly

Rushing
Rushing
Rushing
Rushing
Rushing
Press
Bright
BrightbrightbrightBIG
More
More More In
In
InInInIn
More
InIn
Fill
FillFullFill
Close
Closer
Down
Shhhhhhh

Face
Faces
Face
Colour
Bright
Brightbrightbright
In
In
In
InInIn
Face
Faces
Close
Down
Shhh
Up
Down
Shhh
Up
Down
Shhh
Down
Loud Louder

Soft
Hard
Down
Bright
No
No
No
No
No
Yes!
Feet
Feet there
There That
Feet Foot

Feet
Face

        Wet
        Wet
        Water
        In
        In
        In
        Out
        No
        Nonononono
        A
        Ah
        Ow
        Shh
        Kiss
        Kiss
        Face
        Kiss
        Fill Full Fill
        Down
        Down
        Shhhhhhhh

                Ta Ta Ta Ta Ta Ta
                BBBBBBBBBB
                Face
                Faces
                Smile
                Smiling
                Yes
                Yes
                Yes Yes Yes
                bbbbbbbbb
                Speak:
                RED
                Yes!

redredredredredredredredredredredredredredredredredredredred

Dog is red
Door is red
Floor is red
red red red
Red
Red
Red
Red
Red
Red
Red
Red
Shhh
Red
Red
Red
Red
Red
Fill Full Fill
In
Down

Rrrrr
Red
Face
Mmmmm
Mum
Ma
Ma
Mummy
Ma
Mum
Face
Face
Shhh
Down
Down

MUM
Yes!

Step
Yes
Step
Yes
Yes
Yes Yes Yes
Step
Over
Oops
Oops Oops Oops
Oops
Shhhh
Shh
Oops
Down

MUM
RED
DOG
DA
DAG
DOD
MURRMURRMURRMURRMURRMURRMURR
In
In
Food
FOO
FOOFOOFOO
In
Shhh

Meow
Moo
Woof
Baaa
Tweet
Tweet Tweet Tweet

Bad
No
Bad
Not
No
Not not not No
No
No
NoNoNo
Bad
Shhh
Shh
Down

Bad
Bad
Bad
Bad
(badbadbadbad)

Where's?
There's!
There
Face
MUMMY
Face
DA
DA
DA
DA

Hands
Hands
Hands
Hands
Hands
Hands
Hands
Hands

Oops
Oops
Oops
Kiss
Kisses
Face
Faces
MA
MA MA MA
Oops
Sore
Sore bit
Sore
Kiss
Kisses
(redredredredred)

Boy
Girl
Man
Woman
Dog
Cat
Mouse
Tree
Sky
Grass
Green
Blue
Red
RED
Car
Cars
Tractor
Tractor
123
Onetwothree
12345

Bird
Birds
House
Mummy Daddy
House
Dog
Dogs
Hot
Cold
Oops
Oops
Yes

Good Yes
Bad No
Good Yes
Bad No
No
No
No
No
No
NO
NONONO
NONONONONO

Chick-en
Chick-en
There's you
There's me there's you
There's daddy there's me there's you
There's mummy
There's
Over there
There
House

Out
Out
Wee

Wee-Wee
There
Over there
There's there
In there
Wee-Wee
ppp
Poo
In there
Over there

Who's there
(dogs go-)
Woof
Dog
food there is dog food and people food and cat food (there is a cat in
that house)
And the sky
And the sky
And the sky
And the sky
And the stars at night
And the sun in the day
And the stars at night
And the moon
And

when the big hand and the small hand THREE
I'll come
She'll come
They'll come to get

3

get me
Lunchbox
Sandwiches in my lunchbox
There is peanut butter in the sandwiches
In the sandwiches in the lunchbox in my
Name my name
My name is
Hello my name is

Hello
Mrs Smith
Good morning
Good (yes) morning
Hello my name is
My name is (mummydaddyme)
My name is

Helen Deborah Amy Sarah
Simon Eric Edward Joe Jack
Boys
Girls
Mrs Smith
There
I like don't like
Home hometime Big hand small hand home house mummy daddy me
(bighandsmallhand)

Numbers
Words
Over there
In
I like I don't like
Look like me
Look different (different)
Tuppence Vagina
Vagina
Vagina
In there
In my lunchbox there are
Boys at my table
Boys There are Boys
There are
Willy
Penis
Vagina Vagina Vagina
V V V
The names
Are different

Look different
Mr Casey (boyspenis)
Good morning Good Morning Mr Casey Good morning
My pencil case has
My pencil case has you can smell this one red (red) smells like strawberry
Blue blueberry brown chocolate yellow lemon
Lemon lemon lemon
Lemon is my favourite colour
My mummy says I'm getting a little brother Helen has a little brother
Amy has a bigger brother I have no brother I'm
getting a little brother (my pencil case has)

Smaller than me
Smaller than me I can hold
I can be careful I'm careful Careful
I'm bigger big bigger bigger sister I'm the biggest sister I have a little
brother I can be
Responsible
Responsible
Responsible Grown up I can be Grown Up I have to be
Grown Up now (in my pencil case)
My little brother (boyspenis) David
Balls
Balls
(the testes)
small smaller smallest hands are in my hands These are my hands
These are his hands and I'm

not allowed to watch tv too much it gives you square eyes that's not
true Eric says that's not true that's just what Grown Ups say they lie
like how they lie about everything like how they lie about Santa like
how they lie about
Santa
Santa is real but Mummy and Daddy help him he has so many
houses true
Not true
Kids stuff
Kids
Grown ups Grown Grown

grown ups
Keep it nice
Make it nice for David don't tell
Secrets
Lies
Nice lies
Secrets/Lies Secrets are nice lies and

Some things are
Easier than other things and some things there are things
And things and things
And here's where we are and this is England and this is Britain and
this is Europe and this is America
That's
America Australia Kangaroos kangaRoos upside
Down Paris French Bonjour
There are other things
And other water
There is water
Seas
Oceans
Boats
Planes
Over there
Me mummy daddy david there are other

Joe's grandad died
Joe is sad
Dead Death
Heaven
Heaven?
(Hell)
There is a good place and a bad place
There are other things and other places and
(americaaustraliakangaroo) you can't
To some
I have two grandads and one grandma
I have
Everyone
Everyone dies

Everyone dies
Everyone dies
One day
Not today
Or tomorrow
A long time
A long long way away
Mum says
Everyone (mummydaddydavidme) dies
Everyone dies
Everyone dies
Go and play
Everyone dies
Don't think about it
(everyonedies)
everyonedieseveryonedieseveryonedies
I have a new coat
(everyonedies)
My new coat is green
(everyonedies)
It has pockets
It has zips
I have a new coat
My new coat isveryonedies
This is important there are things that are importantvryonedies and
you have to work hard and if you work hard thendies you will have a
better life there are people with sad livesvryone dies who didn't work
hard and if you want to have a nice life you have to work hard
Test
Testing
Test (testicles)
This is important there are things that are important Maths
I'm not good at maths
Maths
[   ]
I can't
Can't
(important)

Work hard and you'll do well People who work hard do well
Can't
Can't
Can't
Can't
(everyone dies)
Can't
Can't
Can't Can't Can't Won't Don't

like
Dolls
Girls girly girl things
Horses
Horses bite horses can bite you (everyone dies)
Beans
Broccoli
Vegetables?

I like
Robots
Space
Dinosaursvryonedies
(Extinct)
stories books stories I like stories
(lies/secrets/lies)
There are things-
Ice cream

Ice
cream hurts
Ow
OW
My new coat is
Ice cream for holidays
Coke is for holidays
I like coke
Coke is bad for your teeth David isn't allowed coke I'm allowed coke
I'm a grown up responsible girl Woman I'm a Woman Call her a
woman if she wants to be called a woman I think it's sweet
Grown Up

Other families go to america Disney other families go to spain
it's sunny in spain there are places where it's sunny all the time
it's not sunny in the lake district it's wet it rains I like rain
there is water here there is water on the water
Some things you like sometimes some things you like all the times
Holidays
Summer holidays are long longer
Your mother has to work
Your mother has to work sometimes
Sometimes it's just us
(medaddydavid)
After the holidays
I have new shoes
After the holidays you have to
After the holidays you have to go back to

Big school big shoes big bag big books carried onto big bus they told us
year sevens get
Babies get
Year Sevens get pushed around
I used to be big
I used to be the biggest
We
Me and Helen eat our lunch Amy doesn't-
Everyone here smells different There are too many smells here
Everyone smells like their house Every house has a smell Your house
has a smell but you can't smell it
Died Dead Died My Grandad Died No I Didn't Go To The Funeral
(everyonedies) at funerals there are dead people there are dead and
We're not friends anymore
They're not friends anymore so we can't be friends anymore
You can lose friends and you don't get them back
They're not friends anymore because
Boys
Because of boys
There is a boy
They kissed

It's not called kissing no one calls it kissing they got off with each
other it's called
being square are you square
I don't know
If you've never kissed anyone you're square
I did kiss someone but it was on holiday so you wouldn't know them
They're not friends anymore
You can lose friends and not
don't want to be square I think I want to not be square the most in the
world SEX
the most I ever wanted anything is to not be square SEX
I want to not be square please god SEX
Please I don't want to be SEX
It's wet and our teeth are clinking together it hurts he's licking my
filling (can you lick a filling out?) I don't want a boyfriend I just
want to be friends
I don't want to be friends with anyone ever like that
-SIMON TYLER IS MY FIRST KISS-
I can hear myself saying how I liked it I can hear myself saying
things I don't
think I say things I don't think
a lot all the time

I've never done that
Down there
Masturbate
There's a name for It by the way
It's a video everyone has to watch, it's old The Women have full
bushes women don't have bushes anymore
They don't?
Do I have a bush
Not like that
I've never done that
In the bath in bed in the wendy house in the garden on the sofa
behind the sofa in the cupboard I've never done that
everywhere all the time
If you do it for a long time it produces a pleasurable sensation called
an orgasm
Stop having Orgasms

Don't have an Orgasm
Oh you love it so much I bet you're having Orgasms
I never did that In the bath in bed in the wendy house in the garden
behind the sofa in the cupboard under the stairs I've never done it
long enough to get the
(pleasurable sensation called an orgasm)
Oh
Oh
I'm going to break it
I'm going to break myself somehow
(everyonedies)
why can't we have cubicles cubicles to change changing body
your bodies are changing mine isn't changing enough it's broken
I broke it broken blood I'm broken feel broken blood blood bleed
Woman WOMAN ♪ girl you'll be a woman ♪
Why are you crying it's not a big
biggest in school is what they
Big is better because
(pleasurable sensation called an orgasm)
I thought the clitoris
(pleasurable sensation called an orgasm)
But that's not proper Proper SEX WITH BOYS
WITH BOYS
BOYS
PENISES
Everyone has a penis all boys have penises
they're hiding they're just hiding them
(Simon Tyler)
Just hiding them like they're
(Hard-ons)
Did Simon Tyler
(the penis fills with blood causing it to become erect)
Did Simon Tyler get a hard-on
You're giving him a hard-on
Boner
Boners
He's got a boner They've got a boner Got a boner in art Get boners
all the time

> Bonersbonersboners
> There are boners
> Everywhere
> There are boners everywhere I'm surrounded by boners
> gaygaygaylesbianslesbianslesbosdykeslezzaslezzaslezzlezzlezzlet you
> let you if you ask

At Jenna's party you're invited
I'm invited to Jenna's party
I have to wear
I hope when I get home my wardrobe has all new clothes in
I hope when I get home all my old clothes have burnt
Jenna's party
I hope when I
Be careful
We're trusting you
No one else's parents have ever been this scared of a party in the
history of all parents
Big house
Dad be cool
I'm cool
No you're not
Pick you up at eleven but call if you want to leave sooner
I think I'm going to want to stay forever I think parties are meant to
last until the dawn I saw on tv once

THERE IS ALCOHOL AT THIS PARTY

> Everyone's drunk
> Not yet don't be stupid
> It takes time to get drunk
> At christmas I see my mum drunk
> You can get too drunk
> You can become an alcoholic
> Not from one party don't be stupid
> Beer is for boys
> The blue one drink the blue one
> Pretend you have it all the time
> It's very

[

?

]

disappointed in you
trusted you
Your father couldn't come to bed until gone one it took so long to
clean the car
Who knows what you did
In a state like that who knows who did what to you
Boys at your age and older
Older boys
Prey
(I'm Prey Girls are Prey) **RAPE RAPE**
I'm going to buy you an alarm And spray
I don't think the spray is legal
You can buy spray Spray is a thing girls are allowed because of
Boys and their
Penises
Don't talk like that in front of your brother

Jenna's party
I was at Jenna's party
I was so wasted at Jenna's party
I really don't remember I was so Wasted
I was so Wasted at Jenna's party
Got Wasted *at Jenna's party*
Is it true you
Got Wasted *at Jenna's party*
Is it true you
Got Wis it true you

Just ask I bet
Just ask and pretend you're wasted
(got Wasted at jenna's party)
just ask to see it
They'll show
They want to
They want to show

They want us to see
I saw
I saw

At a party
Lots of parties
I've been to lots of parties
I'm the kind of person that goes to parties
And sees
He showed
We saw
Laughed
Don't laugh
Not because
But
Hair everywhere
So many (pubes)
And Doesn't seem that
Wasn't even
Hard-on
If you want to
No thanks

I have seen two penises (four but two don't count)
I have seen two penises I have kissed one boy I think
none of my friends like me
I think the inside of my head is different to the inside of their heads
I think I am different
I think I have no friends even though I say I do
I think people pretend a lot
I think I am pretending all the time

It feels like wood inside a sock but skin
A skin sock
(why they call it a woody sometimes)
I don't feel any different but on the way home I kept my hand in
my pocket the whole time in case my mum could see is that weird?
No I get that
I think Jessica is my best friend
I think Jessica is the only real person in the world

I don't want to do tongues thanks
That's what kissing is
I just think
Just go with it, Jesus
There are wars on tv there are people being blown up like in films on
tv on tv they
say

People say
I'm a slut
So what they can say what they want
I don't want to be a SLUT *though*
I think sluts can make them CUM
Shut up I did my best
Hahaha
Girls who have sex are sluts and boys who have sex are just boys I
think
things are very different all over and no one acts like they are at all
Every film I see has naked boobs but you never see a willy
Jessica's tits TITS *are bigger than mine*
My bum is bigger than Jessica's
Jessica thinks Holden Caulfield is the fittest boy in the world but I
think he seems hard work
I like loud music and sad music
I don't like the words pussy or cunt
Some people are artists There are artists who aren't painters
Art is not just painting
Kurt Cobain killed himself
I don't think I believe in God
I don't believe in God
My parents don't believe in God
I think my Mum does not believe in God I don't know about Dad
I don't know what David believes
I don't believe in Heaven or Hell
I wonder if God is something everyone grows out of
No because look at priests
And there are muslims And there are buddhists and there are jews and
I am not anything and I don't believe in God
I have never been on a plane

Do you feel different?
Not really
Does it hurt
It's sore yeah
How sore
Like a thing is going in where there wasn't a thing going in before
And it was okay it doesn't feel
I didn't have a . . .
(pleasurable sensation called an orgasmcum CUM CUM*)*
Like a thing is going in where there wasn't a thing going in before
Square peg round hole
It hurts but not so much He
wore a johnny (condom) that was flavoured but I didn't put it in my mouth
You're not a virgin anymore
No
But it doesn't Feel feels like

Judy Blume lied to me
Like a thing is going in where there wasn't a thing going in before
Maybe it's different in America
Dave Barnsley
DAVID BARNSLEY
SEX
I am Having Sex with David Barnsley
I am being Fingered by David Barnsley
I wish my first time was with someone with a different
name from my brother
I wish there was a better word than Fingered
I don't think Meg Ryan gets Fingered
fingers are spiky
SEX
I don't want to be on top and I want the lights off
David Barnsley is okay
David Barnsley has not been reported to have the biggest in school
but it comes out the top of my fist when I hold it
He tells me he's worried he'll cum straight away
His breath smells like pasta sauce
Everyone smells like their house

My eyes are used to the dark so I can see the ceiling
The ceiling in his parents' bedroom has wallpaper on it,
how do you wallpaper a ceiling?
Like a thing is going in where there wasn't a thing going in before
Some people do it in the bum
I guess you have special ladders
You're doing well in everything except maths
I hate maths
I will never have to do maths again, no more maths I will
carry a calculator everywhere so I never have to do maths
And some people go to Cambridge And some people go to Oxford
That's another thing
You have to do special
I think some people are classist
Classist
I think some people are Classist
Yes, we know you learnt a new word sweetheart
Racist Classist Homophobe Homophobic
I think you're Homophobic, Dad
I think some of the things they say are wrong I think they're wrong
I think I'll put Newcastle as my second choice
Jessica is going to a different university
If I go here and you go here that's different sides of the country
We can phone and email And message
And my mum says trains are not so expensive
We can visit
I think I'll never meet anyone more perfect than you
I think if I could I'd let you walk around
in my body and I wouldn't be worried
When my parents look at me can they see I've had David Barnsley's
penis inside me
twice
Does it show in how you walk
I think when I asked Dan to stop kissing me he should have
I will never pass my exams and I'll be homeless and die Alone
I don't need a cake you don't have a cake for your eighteenth
I had a cake for my eighteenth
Yeah like a hundred years ago

Alright
They'd probably just invented cake cake had only just come out
Okay thank you
       You're allowed more than one friend to stay if you like you know
              Three B's and a C in General Studies
          no one cares about General Studies (poor mrs hall)
        I'm going to university which is what you're meant to do
                    Are you sure you don't want to take it
                                    No
                      I think you'll miss it when you get there
                                    I don't need it

              I am leaving home
              I am moving away
              This is what people do
              I'll be back
        For christmas for holidays for weekends if I like
              I'm "Leaving Home"
I have a new room with a sink in it a bedroom with a sink in it the
shower is down the hall it's shared shared shower and this is the
number for security and this is your key for your room and your key
for the block as a whole there's no lift I'm afraid your parents can
park up just here to help you unpack but there's a two hour
              maximum period you can stay

                              I have to
                              stay
                              here
           Call us at the weekend so we know how you're getting on
   We won't hug you in front of everyone (please do please hug me
                  please don't let me go everevereverever)
Ever need any just let me know I already have a guy I think when
it's fresher's week they just walk up and down giving out their
                              number
              A drug dealer a drug dealer's
                         DRUGS
                    Most of them are just
Act like you do this all the time even though it feels like your head is
filling up with some kind of something metal I never met a girl
                         stoner before

Is this you?
Yeah
You still had to wear uniform at sixth form
It was a fancy school
I think my family were probably poor
Most people here are not poor
Most people here are not from the north
Most people here seem like they've already been here for years
I have never had a conversation with someone who wasn't white
Some parts of the country are all white and some are not and
Am I a racist by accident
Do I not have to go in every day?
What am I meant to do the whole time?
I want to be a poet
Don't say that it sounds stupid don't say that
I write poetry
I write poetry sometimes
Sometimes I like to write poetry
Sometimes
The parties here smell different to how parties used to smell
(don't just stand in the corner at least look like you're waiting for
someone to get back they'll be back any second i'm just waiting)
Eventually your friends there will be just
as good as the friends you had at school
I only had one friend at school
So then you'll have new friends who are as close as Jessica
Has already got a boyfriend I should have a boyfriend
You'd like him he's into film
("into film")
He's Into Film and he reads a lot
Yeah I have lots of friends here too it's all really cool and I'm writing
lots of poems
You should come and visit
Oh yeah I will just when I'm not so busy maybe there's all- There's so
much-

Your mother is very ill

Your mother is very ill and she's not going to get better

Isn't it a nice room they gave me
(no no no it's not no)

You'll have to all stick together Be kind to each other
Look after your brother

It's raining

why did it have to rain today

this is something that happens to other people

Of course you're going back
No-
She wouldn't want you to miss any more She hated a fuss
Yes-
You have to finish your degree
Yes
You can tell them, the university, they'll make allowances There'll be a procedure
yes

This really isn't good enough, can you talk me through what happened here
What happened is fuck you what's the point just pass me pass pass pass me so I can tell my dad I passed I don't need to know about Chaucer no one needs to know about Chaucer not ever Chaucer is not anything anyone needs to know about ever in the world ever

Dad says you're not doing well at school
I'm fine
Dad says-
You don't have to give me the big sister talk
I know-
I'm fine
Yes

Are you okay?

Yes
Just you're sort of- Wasted
A lot

I'm fine
Everything's fine everything has always been fine fine is the word I
would apply to all of this I have to retake a year but so what anyway
it's not like it even matters
Why do you care anyway
Because we're

friends

Friends
Friends
This is like a sitcom They could make a sitcom about the three of us
living together and people would watch it and think I wish I could
live with those girls in that flat
(Your brother's in trouble again)

> *Our parties are the best because it's exactly the right*
> *amount of people people who come the right amount of*
> *people people who come who came (i don't like to bother*
> *you with it Tell Me Tell Me Always Tell Me) he*
> *he*

HeHeHeHeHeHe is talking to me with that shy smile that I don't
think he knows he does
he like me as much as I

like a film They could make a film about the two of us living together
and people would watch it and think I wish I had what they had
Hands Lips Eyes your brother's in trouble again Looking at Me My
brother David, this is Max Max this is my Dad nice to meet you nice
to meet you a FilmMaker gosh Steven Spielberg Our house is too
small everything here is tiny I don't think it's
people sized And no I don't want to have sex in my childhood
bedroom thanks very much and last time
cystitis cystitis cystitis cystitis would
She like him as much as I like him not the same but see how he makes
me please keep it short dad
Oh don't worry it'll feel short because of all the great jokes I'll be
telling
And obviously the one person who we wish was here
Is this the most obvious song we could have picked has this wedding
happened ten thousand thousand times- why have I worn these pants
I am so uncomfortable and there's no way I'll even want to by the
time we get back to-
I like reading the guidebook because it tells me where to look I don't
know otherwise
Yes we had a wonderful time
I didn't want to call and spoil your honeymoon but I'm afraid your
brother's-

You can't keep doing things like this
It was nothing
You went to Jail
For a few weeks it's not
It doesn't matter how long
I'm fine (fine) *you live your life and I'll live mine how*
Why would they ask where you'll be in five years when obviously
everyone thinks hopefully not still here I hope I'll be exploring
avenues in management and overseeing my own projects and
A BABY
A BABY WILL BE COMING OUT OF ME
IN NINE MONTHS A BABY WILL COME OUT OF ME
You said you were going to paint the room
It doesn't matter what colour it is, she won't notice
I don't think it's sunk in I don't think it'll ever sink in I think
I'm the first woman in the world to not entirely realise a
BABY IS COMING OUT OF ME
I'M GOING TO BREAK SOMETHING SOMETHING'S
WRONG SOMETHING'S WRONG MY SPINE
IS GOING TO
Oh

you're looking right at me

i think i was expecting a thing but you're a person aren't you

I'm just saying it's very good timing you read that article as it means
I'm the one that has to get up to do All The Feeding
Your brother has a job and is doing really well
I don't have a mother I am a mother and I don't have a mother
I need an adult I need a grown up
My nipples feel like they need replacing

My dad is a grandad my dad is old my dad somehow looks smaller
than the baby when he's holding the baby the baby is my baby that's
my daughtereveryonedies I have a daughter Don't drop her
Don't throw her
Don't step on her
Don't sit on her
Don't poison her
Don't choke her
Don't set her alight
Don't electrocute her
Don't drown her
Don't cut her into bits no
No I want you to keep working on your film I'm too tired to do much
else than sit with her anyway you're very talented don't say that keep
going you need to use this time because once I'm back at work
Back at work
Back at work
Back in this car at this time of day with this radio I don't even like
this show why do I listen to this every day driving to work
Driving to work
Driving to work
Driving to work
Driving to work
Driving to work
Driving to work
Driving to work
Driving to work
Driving to work
Driving to work
Driving to work
Driving to work
Driving to work
Driving to work
Driving to work
Driving to work
Driving to work
Driving to work
That's called Motor Skill and she's meant to be better at it by now
So she's clumsy she's our lovely clumsy girl

Driving to work
Driving to work
Driving to work
Driving to work
Driving to work
Driving to work
Driving to work
Driving to work
Driving to work
Driving to work
Driving to work
Driving to work
Driving to work
Driving to work
Driving to work
Driving to work
Driving to work

> *I always thought we'd have three*
> *We can barely manage with one*

Driving to work

> *The cost of childcare is obscene actually obscene*

Driving to work
Driving to work
Driving to work
Driving to work
Driving to work
Driving to work
Driving to work
Driving to work
Driving to work
Driving to work
Driving to work
Driving to work
Driving to work
Driving to work
Driving to work

Your father and I just think-
He doesn't think anything, it's you it's all just you
and what you think

Driving to work
Driving to work
Driving to work
Driving to work
Driving to work
Driving to work
Driving to work
Driving to work
Driving to work
Driving to work
Driving to work
Driving to work
Driving to work
Driving to work
Driving to work
Driving to work

You have to be reasonably realistic with what
grades you're going to get
You said I can go wherever I want
You can but you have to-

Driving to work
Driving to work
Driving to work
Driving to work
Driving to work
Driving to work
Driving to work
Driving to work
Driving to work

Are you sure you don't want to take it
No
I think you'll miss it when you get there
I don't need it

Driving to work
Driving to work
Driving to work

Call us once a week that's all we want
Okay-
I love you
Mum please-

Driving to work
Driving to work
Driving to work
Driving to work
Driving to work
Driving to work
Driving to work
Driving to work
Driving to work
Driving to work
Driving to work
Driving to work I have to leave my brother has died

He was doing really well but I don't know something just
(look after your brother)

(look after your brother)

(look after your brother)

I'm sorry Mum
thank you sweetheart

Driving to work

Driving to work

Driving to work
Driving to work
Driving to work
Driving to work
Driving to work
Driving to work
Well I don't see why you can't just work on it here that's what the
spare room's for

Driving to work
Driving to work
Driving to work
Driving to work
Driving to work
Driving to work
Driving to work
Driving to work
Driving to work
Driving to work
Driving to work
Driving to work
Driving to work
Driving to work
Nothing's happened we just don't particularly want to be married
anymore

I don't see why I have to tell her-
Because she probably already knows It's extremely fucking obvious
No, he's not a bad person He was very talented when he was younger
He's still talented,
you're right

Driving to work
Driving to work
Driving to work
Driving to work
Driving to work
Driving to work
Driving to work
Driving to work
Driving to work
Driving to work
Driving to work
Driving to work
Driving to work
Driving to work

A poet? God
I don't think I've ever once had a poetic thought
Driving to work
Driving to work
Driving to work
Driving to work
Driving to work
Driving to work
Driving to work
Driving to work
Driving to work

I still have friends If you're close enough with your
friends you don't have to see them
Or call them
Driving to work
Driving to work
Driving to work
Driving to work

Driving to work
Driving to work
    I can't call the post office because they'll ask what it is I'll just buy
        another They're so expensive though and there's
        nothing to be ashamed of I'm a grown woman with perfectly
        normal

Driving to work
Driving to work
Driving to work
Driving to work
Driving to work
Driving to work
Driving to work
    Did you make the cake? Oh, it's from Marks?
    Am I a terrible person for expecting better cake after thirty-six years
        of working here Yes yesyes absolutely
        So much time now you've got
        So much time now
    To do all those things you always wanted to do and I don't remember
        the things I wanted to do and
    Retirement's the best kept secret that's what I've always said the best
        kept secret
        So many things to do
        To do
        That's right
        Did you ever consider getting a cat Dad
        A cat? No, I'm not a cat person
    (Do you blame me for not being able to talk to him I could never talk
    to him he didn't want to be talked to I didn't try hard enough) and
AND WE'RE GETTING MARRIED
Marriage is a wonderful thing-
You say
I don't regret marrying your father
You think it's too soon
I think it's right if you think it's right he seems very nice tall broad
    Sex it must be sex sex can make all sorts of things seem like good
    ideas her choice her choice I don't I can't

Dad says he's really happy
That's good
He's going to write a speech
Well we're all still waiting for his film
That's mean
It is, I'm sorry
People don't give me leaflets anymore I walk past people promoting
things and they don't see me as a reasonable home for their flyer I am
not a target demographic I don't know when that
happened I never see a woman my age on tv or in a film having a
good time I never see a woman my age I never see women my age
maybe they don't see me either we're all just as invisible to each other
as we are to everyone else
Dress Hat Photos Photos Photos Speech Toast Speech Toast Speech
Toast Sore palms Cake Dance Drunk Drunker Bed
I think he's probably a moron but he's a nice
enough moron I suppose
Your granddad's died but I don't expect you to come back for the
funeral if you're busy
Probably for the best much longer and
Ash
You were the biggest man in the world and now you're just ash you
used to step over buildings and I don't know what all this is I see
myself in photographs I see people in photographs and I'm
For the poetry? fewer people here than I supposed there would be
even fewer than I guessed there would
be at a poetry evening at a library in a small town most older than
me here because they've even less than me
to do
this I used to want to do this is this what I wanted to do or did I just
like the
Idea
Poem Poem Poem Poem Poem Applause
There are crumbs under my seat
Poem Poem Poem Applause
Published apparently I suppose I think I could maybe
Yes thank you Yes I used to Yes maybe at the next-
It's weekly It's going to be weekly This is Bill I forget your surname

Teacher Teacher at school new to town English "The Local Scene"
Hahaha
Maybe I'll see you at the next
evening
Everything feels
clammy Everyone can hear my thighs sticking together there is no
microphone rooms this small don't need microphones

~POEM~

Do you remember me Oh yes I'm Bill Lowell I teach at The teacher
yes that's right I
Loved Your Poem
Thank you so much I was so nervous
You didn't seem to be
I was so nervous I've never done this even when I was Yes why not I
could show you the places to be I could show you some things it's only
a small

Died doesn't say passed away says died she died
I'm sorry yes my brother [   ]
That's very
Late it's very late do you think he has very very very blue bluest eyes
and Lips lipslips
can't go in a shop like that there are no women in the photos in the
window who look like me I Can't ridiculous
Oh
Oh
OH
Well-
That was-
Yes-
I hardly knew what I was
Want to wear a dress not one of those suits like old Old Ladies wear
Old Old I'm Weddings are for the Young not
No your father's not invited
Because it wouldn't be appropriate
Of course he's family
I would really like you to be there
Of course I do

Dress Photo Speech Toast Applause Cake Dance Bed
Scotland Read Reading
Talking Talking Talking Talking Talking Talking
a valve opened somewhere
Does he love me more or less or just the same as his first wife do I love
him more than my first I feel I love him more than anything or
anyone today
I can't force her to talk to me
She's welcome here whenever she'd like to yes I'm sure your parents
separating but I lost my mother and (look after your) brother and I
didn't stop I don't think I'm
being the stubborn one here
Here
Here she is
Here she is!
Don't cry
Don't cry, I love you, don't cry
It wasn't so long don't cry I forgive you I forgive you I forgive
everything I'm the great forgiver
It's so nice to see you I see you I see you I can see you until you're
back in my arms right back just a speck a tiny speck carrying a tiny
speck speck that's you
due
in June In June she's due in June a summer baby a new baby for the
summer (read somewhere about population absolute crisis point
everyone dies) a grandma me The Grandma I'm Grandma not
granny far too old Grandma please
can I be a Grandma can I be a Grandma's House can I be that
house my grandparents were not that house so much maybe I can be
me be
It's happening It's happening now now now Quick Quick keys keys
can never find keys where are the KEYS
Hi hihihi
Hi-

hello

there's a thread running from me
to you

Is this what I imagined life was Yes I suppose
walks
Lots of walks Long walks
Prams Pushchairs Cakes with Candles
Are these my images or ones we're all given
　　You can't control what she does or where she goes you of all people
　　　　　　　　　　　　　　　　　　　　should know
　　　　　　　　　　　　　　It's the way she talks to me
　　　　　　　　　　　　　　　　　　　　　　Well
　　　　　　　　　　　　　I never spoke to you like that
　　　　　　　　　　　　　　　　　　　　　Well!

　　　　　　　　Look after yourself
　　　　　　　　You know you can't
　　　　　　　　I won't be fussed over
　　　　　　　　Well the doctors-
　　　　　　　　I'm sick of doctors
　　　　Well I should think you are but that doesn't change
　　　　　　　The finish on the casket if you'd like a different hue
No that's fine this is all fine and the flowers- He wasn't fussed about
flowers Why would anyone want to be buried not (burnt) cremated I
told him he was mad but that's what he wanted and everyone else
　　　　　Everyone always looking at me out the
　　　　　corner of their eye as if I've never
　　　　　　　　I'm fine

　　　　　　　　　　　　　　　　　　Fine
　　　　　　Everything's fine everything's always fine
　　　　　　everyone dies and it's fine and it's fine and
　　　　　　the house will be quieter but I'll always have
And what do you think you saw
I told you
But you didn't-
I said I came home and my brother was sitting on the sofa There

Your brother-
David Was his name
I remember- But-
Stop talking to me like that
Like what
Like I'm a Lonely Old Woman seeing things
It's just-
I know how it sounds but I'm telling you I'm not interested in
whether ghosts exist or where whatever goes or what it means or
anything what to do with it I'm not going to bring people here with
machines to scan the place for ectojism
Plasm mum
I'm just telling you what I saw which was my
brother sitting on the sofa Looking at me
Did he talk to you
No and what would he say nothing to say nothing to say likely look
after your brother I tried I tried to look after you I think of you all the
time I can't get through a day without thinking of you I think of you
I think
I think you're the most important person in my life and you're dead
and I never spoke to you much when you were alive and I would
understand it if you felt the need to haunt me if that's what that was
what this is haunt me all you like I don't mind it'd be nice to have
someone to watch the tv with of an evening time

        Isn't really on your side here (everyonedies) and any
        operations we could do would only buy you a little more
        time and it'd be time you wouldn't enjoy much either
                Well you can't just
                I'll do as I like it's my life-
                    But they
                      They
  told me what They told me and that's that there's no use getting in a
                  tizz about it-
                      Mum
   Mummummummummummummothermothermothermother
   mothergrandmothergrandgrandmamumumumumumumu
        mumumumumumumumumumnnnnnn
  not going to one of those places no matter what you say

but it's the only place they can
I know I'm a burden
You're not a burden
A burden I'm a burden (everyone dies) a burden that can't won't
See it's not so bad the window looks out onto the lawns there
Yes lovely thank you
never liked gardening gardens flowers don't understand the appeal
an utterly shallow exercise as far as I can see what do you do once
you've made a garden just sit and stare at it and realise your head's
as empty as it was before
Ah!
AH!
No don't bring her let her see me in here too much let her think of me
in better shape I really
don't mind David's here with me
Well let her think that if it helps what am I supposed to
Mum I love you
Mum I love you
I love you, Mum
I love you I love you I love you I love you
I love you I love you I love you
I'm so embarrassed I wish I could tell them to leave and not watch
the next bit whatever the next bit is dark
It's dark

It's dark
IT'S DARK wetwetnesswetwetmyselfhorribledon't looknoNONO
quiet always quiet here so
quiet
see the corners melting can you
think i had a good life but its hard to tell really i don't have anything
to compare
might have been happier at times but then probably everyone could
have
regrets i have regrets (look after your brother) it's fine to have regrets
i'm allowed No Regrets is what people say but that's a fridge magnet
i think
oh OH there are no edges to anything

*driving to work can't see the sides of the road all slipping away from
me i have a new coat stop kissing me and there's wallpaper on the
ceiling
on the ceiling it's so strange there's red
Red Rushing Close Closer And I can smell mum's
Jumper
Can't
hands and hands my hands press pressing
this is all very
red red rushing In Red
Rushing
Rushing
Rushing
Rushing
-*

With thanks to The MacDowell Colony, where this was written.

www.ingramcontent.com/pod-product-compliance
Ingram Content Group UK Ltd.
Pitfield, Milton Keynes, MK11 3LW, UK
UKHW020706280225
455688UK00012B/299

9 781350 168169